GOOD TO GREAT EMPLOYEE

PRAVEEN KUMAR

notionpress
.com

INDIA • SINGAPORE • MALAYSIA

ISBN

Paperback 979-8-89724-956-5

Hardcase 979-8-89777-644-3

Dedicated to

My mentors and coaches, whose wisdom and guidance have been invaluable; to my wonderful wife, whose love and support sustain me; and to my two amazing children, who inspire me every day.

Praveen Kumar is a seasoned professional who began his career at the Indian Space Research Organization (ISRO) as a scientist after completing his postgraduate degree in engineering from the University of Delhi. After six years of contributing to India's space program, he transitioned to the private sector, gaining extensive experience in various product design companies. Currently, he works for a leading product design multinational corporation.

Praveen has honed his management expertise under the guidance of mentors and coaches, alongside a deep passion for continuous learning through books. His diverse experiences and insights into engineering, design, and leadership have shaped his unique perspective, making him a thought leader in his field. In addition, he has developed expertise across various technical fields, authoring more than 20 technical papers and securing many patents that highlight his innovative contributions.

A regular speaker at conferences and industry events, Praveen has shared his knowledge with diverse audiences, earning widespread recognition. He is also a dedicated mentor to professionals across different fields and organizations, helping them navigate challenges and achieve their goals. His commitment to learning and sharing knowledge reflects his enduring passion for personal and professional growth.

Contents

Disclaimers

The ideas expressed in this book are the author's own and do not reflect the views, opinions, or endorsement of his employer or any other organization or individual.

The names, examples, and stories in this book are entirely fictitious. Any resemblance to actual persons, living or dead, or real events is purely coincidental.

A Note from Author

I still vividly remember the first day of my career at the Indian Space Research Organisation (ISRO). I came in with a heart full of dreams – dreaming of making a significant contribution to my country and society, while striving to grow and excel in my career. I had a vague understanding of what professional growth meant at that point in time. All I took with me was the theoretical knowledge I had acquired during college.

I dedicated considerable effort over time to bridge this gap, gaining knowledge not only from literature but also through interactions with remarkable individuals in my surroundings. I was fortunate enough to have outstanding leaders, mentors, coaches, colleagues and mentors who generously shared their knowledge and experience. Each interaction and shared insight became a valuable lesson, helping me navigate challenges and grow both personally and professionally.

This book is the culmination of my learning from over two and a half decades of experience. I have endeavoured to present my insights in a raw, honest, and concise format. To respect your time, I tried to keep the book brief and to the point, allowing you to absorb its essence without feeling overwhelmed.

The content of this book is structured into 35 days, with each day's material intended to be read one day at a time. This daily approach provides you with the opportunity to reflect on the lessons, relate them to your own work and life situations, and discover practical ways to apply these learning effectively.

I owe my deepest gratitude to my parents, wife, kids, managers, mentors, coaches, colleagues, and mentees, from whom I have learned so much—and continue to learn every day. Without their influence, this book would not have been possible.

I sincerely hope you relish this book and find it valuable on your own journey.

Your thoughts and feedback are important to me. Please feel free to share them with me via email.

Praveen Kumar
getintouch.praveenk@gmail.com

Day-1

Why Didn't You Ask Me!!!

"You should have asked me... What was the hurry... This is not what I asked for... Why didn't you check with me?"

Many of us have heard these comments from our managers at some point.

Employees often interpret these types of comments from managers in a negative way, feeling frustrated or undervalued. Over the years, I've heard them explain this by citing various reasons, such as:

"Managers need to show they're contributing, even when they're not."

"Managers feel the need to prove they're in charge."

"Managers themselves aren't clear about what they want."

While there may be truth to these perceptions, I believe the core issue often boils down to one thing: communication.

Despite the fact that many corporate employees are trained in communication skills, practical, day-to-day communication techniques are often overlooked.

Let's look at Suresh's story.

Suresh, an engineer with over eight years of experience in hardware design, was responsible for validating hardware and generating reports in his company. His manager typically assigned tasks to the team, and once the reports were completed, they would be sent to the manager for final review. The manager would then coordinate with other teams and send the reports to the customers.

One day, Suresh's manager asked him if he could finish an important report by Thursday, 5 PM, as he would be going out of town, and the report was critical for a key customer. Despite Suresh's efforts, the report wasn't ready on time. It was Friday at 10 AM when the work was finally completed.

Suresh hesitated to inform his manager about the delay, thinking it might not be well received. Wanting to show initiative, he located the customer's email and sent the report directly to the customer, believing his manager would appreciate the proactive effort in his absence. Suresh rationalized that swift action was better than inaction, convincing himself that addressing the customer's needs promptly was the right decision.

However, when Suresh's manager returned on Monday, he was visibly upset. The report had been intended for review before being sent, with specific instructions to format it and remove certain content. His manager told him, **"You should have asked me before sending it**." Suresh, feeling his effort to help had gone unappreciated, grew increasingly frustrated. He thought his manager was being overly critical and accused him of nitpicking, despite the extra work he had done to meet the customer's needs.

Now let's look at different scenario in the same story.

On Thursday morning, Suresh realized he wouldn't be able to complete the report by the 5 PM deadline. Concerned, he called his manager to inform him about the delay, explaining that the report would be ready by Friday morning instead. His manager appreciated the early notice and replied, "Good that you informed me now. Let me check with the other team's manager to see if he can cover for me and handle the coordination this week."

A few minutes later, the manager called Suresh back with an update. "The other team's manager has agreed to step in and coordinate for me this week. I'll send you the report format and his contact details over email. Please ensure the content is formatted correctly before sending it out."

After returning to the office on Monday, Suresh's manager sent an email expressing gratitude to the other team's manager for stepping in during his absence. He also acknowledged Suresh's efforts, highlighting how he had ensured the critical report was handled smoothly in his absence.

Golden words: Aligning with your manager's working style and understanding their requirements is crucial for building a strong relationship.

I Thought... A Warning Sign?

"I thought you were sending that email"... "I thought it was not that urgent"... This type of reasoning is all too common in the corporate world.

Let's break down what's happening here.

Person A had one set of expectations, while Person B operated on a completely different assumption. These disconnect highlights a common challenge in collaboration: the risks posed by assumptions. Often, these unspoken beliefs become a major source of project delays or customer dissatisfaction, underscoring the need for clear communication.

In most corporate environments, employees are trained to set **SMART** goals—**S**pecific, **M**easurable, **A**chievable, **R**elevant, and **T**ime-Bound. However, a common oversight is limiting this approach to long-term, annual objectives. While SMART goals are often associated with strategic planning, their principles are just as critical for smaller, everyday tasks. Even seemingly straightforward activities, such as sending a purchase order to a vendor, benefit from the same level of precision and clarity. Applying SMART criteria across all levels of work can help eliminate misunderstandings and foster smoother workflows.

Let's look at Suresh's story.

Suresh worked in the procurement team of a large multinational company. During a daily morning meeting about a critical project, the project manager assigned action items to the team. One of Suresh's responsibilities was to release a purchase order (PO) to PK Engineering. The team discussed the next steps, reached a consensus, and the meeting concluded.

The following day, the project manager asked, "Suresh, has the PO been released?"

Suresh replied, "Not yet—I thought it would be fine to release it in the next day or two."

The project manager frowned and said, "This is unacceptable; it's a high-priority task. Now the project is delayed by a day."

The instruction seemed straightforward: release the PO. However, if Suresh had applied SMART goal principles, he would have asked a simple yet crucial question: "By when do you need the PO released?" That single clarifying question could have prevented the delay entirely.

Sentences that begin with "I thought" often indicate a misunderstanding or a lack of clear communication.

In this scenario, the principles of SMART goals apply not just to Suresh but also to the project manager. While assigning action items, the project manager should have specified a clear timeline for releasing the PO (time-bound) and confirmed its feasibility (achievable). This proactive approach would have avoided the delay and ensured that expectations were aligned from the outset.

This story underscores the importance of applying SMART principles to all levels of task delegation and execution, even for seemingly straightforward actions.

A simple yet effective guardrail is to avoid situations where your response might begin with, "I thought..."

Golden words: Be mindful of your communication; think before using "I thought". Consider taking proactive steps that can help you avoid situations where that phrase becomes necessary.

———————— •◇• ————————

Day-3

Feedback is the Best Career Gift

"You should increase your contribution," "You need to work on your communication," or "It would be beneficial to improve your stakeholder management skills."

Many of us have received feedback like this and often react uncomfortably. Our instinct may be to justify our actions, explaining why we believe we are already meeting expectations or comparing ourselves to others to prove we're doing better.

I've seen feedback lead to significant consequences, including job stress, resignation, or even termination.

Let's explore Matt's story.

Matt was a sincere, hardworking, and results-oriented employee. He was satisfied with his work, and everything seemed to be going well. However, during his latest performance review, his manager pointed out that he needed to improve his presentation skills. Matt responded that he delivered most of the presentations without receiving any complaints from stakeholders.

Yet, his manager insisted, "I agree, but you need to up your game."

After that meeting, Matt struggled to focus on his work, feeling that all his hard work for the company was in vain. He even spoke to some colleagues who fueled his frustration by speculating that the manager was looking for reasons to justify not promoting him or to give him a lower pay raise.

As a result, Matt's performance began to decline, and he started seeking job opportunities outside the company.

Now, let's change the scenario.

After listening carefully to the feedback, Matt thanked his manager and committed to improve. He asked for tips to expedite his progress. The manager suggested some training sessions and recommended a few mentors known for their excellent presentation skills.

Matt completed the recommended trainings, connected with the two of the suggested mentors, and kept his manager informed about his progress. He felt he had significantly improved his presentation skills through the trainings and the guidance provided by his mentors. A year later, Matt was promoted to a role with greater responsibilities, where he was required to present to senior executives and customers.

During a one-on-one meeting, Matt asked his manager why he had been selected for the promotion.

The manager explained that there were three potential candidates, each needing to refine 1-2 skills to be a good fit for the role. However, Matt made the most rapid progress, impressing management with his development. The manager expressed pride in having Matt on his team.

Golden words: Always accept feedback, even if it's based on perception rather than fact.

Wrong Feedback... Why to Bother!

At some point in our careers, most of us have received feedback that we believed was inaccurate or misguided. Whether it's about our work performance, behaviour, or a specific skill set, we may feel confident that the assessment doesn't align with our own understanding or perception of our abilities. In those moments, it's natural to question the feedback or even dismiss it. However, how we respond to feedback—whether we agree with it or not—can significantly impact our growth and the opportunities that may come our way.

Let's consider Matt's story.

Matt was a software engineer at a service company. He was intelligent, hardworking, and skilled. During a one-on-one meeting, Matt received feedback from a senior colleague, Mahi, suggesting that he should improve his technical skills in a specific area. Matt believed he was already performing well in that area.

Matt was upset upon hearing this feedback and immediately told Mahi that he disagreed. He cited examples of being praised in meetings and trainings he had conducted on the same topic. He left the meeting without thanking Mahi for the feedback. Later, Matt escalated the issue to his manager and shared his frustration with other employees, criticizing Mahi's behaviour.

As a result, Matt's relationship with Mahi deteriorated.

Now, let's imagine a different scenario.

After receiving the feedback, Matt thanked Mahi and asked for more details on what he could improve and if Mahi had any suggestions. Mahi recommended an expert within the company and offered to connect Matt with them. The meeting ended on a positive note.

A week later, Matt met with Mahi again to understand why Mahi felt he needed to improve in that area. Mahi explained that during a recent important project discussion, no one had suggested Matt's name for the work, which Mahi believed would have been a great opportunity for him. Knowing that Matt had some expertise in the area, Mahi wanted to help him avoid missing out on similar opportunities in the future. He further advised Matt to connect with domain experts both inside and outside the company for better visibility. Matt realized he wasn't well-connected and employees in related areas were not aware of his skills. He thanked Mahi for the advice.

From that point, Matt's respect for Mahi grew, and he even requested Mahi to be his career mentor.

Golden words: Feedback should always be embraced, as it provides an opportunity to view yourself from others' perspective.

———— •◇• ————

Day-5

It Was a Perception!

Matt was a mechanical engineer at a company specializing in designing parts for the aerospace industry, and he consistently performed well above average. A forward-thinking employee, Matt stayed updated on industry trends and emerging technologies to sharpen his skills. He also had two mentors—one within the company and another external—whom he consulted regularly. Matt typically exceeded his goals and felt confident in his overall performance.

One day, during a 1:1 conversation with Mahi, a peer of his manager, Matt received some unexpected feedback. Mahi suggested that he needed to improve his communication skills. This feedback took Matt by surprise, as his own manager had often praised his communication abilities. Though surprised, Matt remained professional and thanked Mahi for the feedback.

Following this conversation, Matt sought additional feedback from a few of his colleagues, though he chose not to mention Mahi's comments. His co-workers reassured him that his communication style was clear, concise, and effective, which only added to his confusion. Determined to resolve the matter, Matt approached his manager for clarity. His manager echoed the feedback from his colleagues, stating, "Like everyone, there's always room for improvement, but I don't see any major gaps. Your communication, whether technical or non-technical, is strong."

While reassured by this feedback, Matt remained determined to ensure there were no overlooked areas of improvement. He took it upon himself to read more about communication techniques and areas for growth, eager to refine his skills even further.

About two months later, Matt brought up the topic with his mentor, still thinking about Mahi's feedback and his efforts to improve. He was eager to hear what his mentor thought of the steps he'd taken since. As Matt explained Mahi's feedback and how he had reflected on his communication style, making subtle adjustments along the way, his mentor listened intently.

After a brief pause, the mentor smiled and said, "You handled this the right way, Matt. Instead of reacting defensively, you embraced the feedback and took action." Matt felt a wave of relief, but his mentor wasn't finished.

"However," the mentor continued, "there's something more you need to understand. Feedback isn't always just about your actual performance; it's often shaped by how people perceive you. And perceptions can be just as influential as reality. Managing perception is as important as addressing real gaps." The mentor leaned in, speaking more seriously now. "Perceptions can be shaped by a single interaction or accumulate from various sources over time. Sometimes, all it takes is one moment for someone to form an opinion that sticks, even if it doesn't fully reflect your true abilities. While feedback highlights areas to improve, perception management ensures that those improvements are visible and well understood by others."

This conversation helped Matt recognize the importance of not only refining his communication but also ensuring that others perceived his strengths as he intended.

Golden words: Effective perception management is just as important as managing feedback.

———— •◇• ————

Day-6

Team in a Silo!!

One of the biggest career mistakes is failing to regularly update and align with your management and stakeholders. Many employees adopt a "give me the work, and I'll finish it" mindset, particularly in highly technical teams. While they may complete the tasks as instructed, the outcomes may not always be as favourable as expected.

As we progress in our careers and move up the management ladder, each subsequent level gains a deeper understanding of the bigger picture—often revealing a perspective that differs significantly from our own, which is shaped by the limited data we possess.

Let's look at Suresh's story.

Suresh was a hardworking and talented manager who led a team of equally dedicated engineers and designers in a motorbike company. His team was responsible for chain mechanism. Suresh's manager got a task to design world class motor bike, he discussed with his teams and made a solid plan. The work was distributed among multiple teams, including electrical, industrial design, wheels and chain, and engine.

As Suresh began working on the design, he preferred to work in isolation, believing that communicating with other teams would interfere with his progress and is a waste of time. He was determined to outperform his peers to advance his career more quickly. Consequently, he hesitated to share his thought process, convinced it was superior to that of others.

After a few months, the prototype design was ready for its first assembly test, and Suresh was excited, confident that his team had delivered the best design. However, after spending several days on the assembly test, team discovered that Suresh's design did not fit with the other parts. While the other teams had engaged in discussions and optimized specifications as they progressed and learned about the overall design, Suresh chose to ignore those meetings and relied solely on emails for updates. As a result, he missed key points that were discussed in both formal and informal settings.

This situation raises important questions: Is Suresh a bad manager or simply an employee lacking the right skills? The answer lies not in his talent, but in his approach to collaboration. Suresh's desire to make faster career progress drove him to work in isolation, believing that he could outshine his peers by independently delivering superior work. However, this strategy backfired, as it ultimately hindered his ability to align with the larger team goals.

Maintaining good relationships with stakeholders, management, and partner groups is essential for achieving better results and advancing in one's career. By recognizing the value of communication and teamwork, Suresh could not only enhance his design processes but also ensure his team's efforts align with the broader project objectives. Embracing collaboration could have enabled him to leverage the strengths of his colleagues, leading to more innovative solutions and a faster path to success.

Golden words: Working in isolation does not lead to faster progress in the long run, as your ideas may fail to strengthen and align with those of others.

Raise Hand...

Many individuals are diligently striving to progress in their careers, and a frequent recommendation from supervisors and mentors is to "raise your hand." This expression encourages taking the initiative and actively seeking out opportunities that arise.

However, this guidance can be perplexing, as many times individuals don't know what steps to take and if our actions are appropriate.

The first thing to remember is that "nothing is free"; everything has a cost associated with it.

Once you decide to take action, consider the following questions to guide you:

- Why do you want to differentiate yourself, and what price are you willing to pay for this? The cost could be in the form of extra work hours, attending additional meetings, or collaborating with someone you may not particularly like.

- Each company has its own environment and values, so take the time to learn what is valued in your organization and what is not.

- Think about your support system—your direct manager, senior management, mentors, peers, and colleagues in other groups—who can assist you along the way.

Another challenge is that many of us are unaware of the power of raising our hands to seize opportunities and how to do it effectively. This often leads to missed chances for growth and recognition. Knowing when and how to volunteer can significantly impact our careers and help us stand out in a competitive environment.

Let's explore this through Peter's story.

Peter manages a team of 10 talented engineers, which includes three hardware engineers, three test engineers, and four automation engineers. All of them are equally hardworking and dedicated. Matt, a member of the team, was encouraged by his mentor to step up and take initiative. Taking the advice to heart, he began actively seeking opportunities and taking decisive actions.

During a staff meeting, Peter expressed his desire to reduce the time spent in meetings and enhance their efficiency. He then asked if anyone would be interested in helping with this initiative. After a brief pause, Matt raised his hand and expressed his interest in contributing. Peter replied that they could discuss it further after the meeting.

Following this, Matt collaborated with Peter, gathering feedback through emails and conducting short meetings, as well as informal discussions during tea and lunch breaks. In total, Matt spent about four to five hours on these activities. He consolidated the feedback and prepared a presentation with recommendations based on his findings. Peter then discussed Matt's recommendations with other managers and higher management. Later, Matt was invited to present proposed ideas in various forums.

Six months later, Matt's work was recognized by the group VP during an all-hands meeting.

Consider this: by raising his hand and investing only 5-6 hours over six months, Matt earned recognition that was difficult to achieve through his regular assigned tasks. His reputation was solidified as an employee who is:

- Proactive

- Thinks beyond his immediate team

- Capable of contributing beyond day-to-day responsibilities

This is the power of "raising hand" which can put you ahead of your peers.

Here are a few examples of situations where you can raise your hand:

1. Organizing various events

2. Training other employees

3. Participating in short-term initiatives to reduce costs, conducting specific surveys, or assisting HR in implementing new systems

4. Supporting a project that is running short on resources

5. Procuring items for your team or lab

Golden words: Raising your hand is a powerful tool for accelerating your career progress—when done correctly.

Acknowledge Help to Get Help!

None of us enjoy office politics, yet it can be challenging to avoid at times. Much of office politics arises from the perception that someone is taking advantage of others. Often, these feelings originate from misunderstandings or misinterpretations.

What's the solution? The best approach is to maintain a clean and healthy environment around oneself.

Suresh, a software engineer at a multinational company designing refrigerators for the global market, was sincere and hardworking. His manager appreciated his contributions, yet Suresh felt dissatisfied with the atmosphere around him.

Let's examine Suresh's working style and the atmosphere around him. His role requires data from various team members and colleagues. Unfortunately, he often does not receive this data without repeated requests, forcing him to constantly remind others. He sends emails, Instant Messages (IM), and tries to catch people in their cubicles or corridors when he sees them.

This becomes even more challenging with teams located in different parts of the country and abroad.

When he finally receives the data, he often highlights the delays caused by its late arrival, believing that this will help others appreciate the importance of timely responses and ensure he receives the data on time in the future with less effort. However, this approach fails to yield the desired results, leaving Suresh feeling trapped in a non-performing and political environment.

From the perspective of those working with Suresh, the situation looks quite different. They feel that he constantly asks for data without considering the challenges they face. They see him as selfish and believe he takes advantage of their hard work. Moreover, some of them think he is simply riding on their efforts without contributing his fair share.

In this scenario, everyone is justified in their views.

Now, let's identify what's missing here. Suresh is failing to:

1. Build a personal connection with the teams that are critical to his work; he is showing interest in the data rather than in the individuals behind the data.

2. Recognize the contributions of the teams providing him with information.

A few basic actions can significantly improve this situation, which may seem daunting. Here are some suggestions for Suresh:

1. Spend time with the individuals who are directly or indirectly critical to his work. Try to understand their work and challenges faced by them.

2. Engaging in small talk during tea breaks or sharing lunch table can work wonders.

3. Send a thank-you note after receiving data instead of highlighting delays and their impact.

4. Write an appreciation note to the manager of the employee who helped, copying the employee on the message.

5. Acknowledge how the success of projects depends on these supportive teams whenever he has the opportunity to discuss project outcomes, such as during completion celebrations or project-related awards.

Golden words: One must master the art of recognizing and appreciating the support of others to ascend to greater heights in their career.

———————— •◇• ————————

Day-9

Thanking Someone for Asking for Help!!

Matt is a star employee who consistently excels, no matter the challenges within his team. Even when projects are canceled, his success remains unaffected as he plays a key role in multiple initiatives. His ability to navigate setbacks with ease leaves many colleagues wondering how he attracts so many opportunities.

Here's his secret: years ago, Matt was asked to help on another team's project for a few weeks. When the project concluded, he thanked the team for the opportunity, expressing how it broadened his knowledge of projects and technologies outside his own team. He also conveyed his eagerness to contribute to future opportunities. He sent a note of appreciation to the managers and leaders of both teams, building valuable connections.

A few months later, one of his new contacts asked if he could assist with a project in need of extra resources. It turned out he was recommended by someone from the previous project he had helped. Though busy, Matt went the extra mile, working nights and weekends to support this new project for several months.

Matt has been following this approach for years, and the results speak for themselves:

1. He has a deeper understanding of projects beyond his own team compared to his peers.

2. He stays informed about which technologies and types of projects are gaining traction within the company.

3. He's built a strong, diverse network across the organization.

4. He has developed numerous adjacent skills beyond his core expertise.

5. He consistently works on high-priority projects, regardless of what's happening within his immediate team.

6. His 360-degree feedback is consistently excellent, giving him a clear advantage over his peers.

The secret lies in Matt's approach. He not only delivers results but builds relationships, turning every project—successful or not—into a learning and networking opportunity. His proactive attitude, coupled with a genuine curiosity about different aspects of the business, ensures that new doors are always opening for him. It's not just his skills that make him stand out, but his willingness to go the extra mile and stay connected long after a project wraps up. His secret weapon is his unwavering gratitude towards peers, managers, and even juniors who provide him with new or diverse opportunities.

Golden words: Thanking those who ask for your help has the similar impact as expressing gratitude to those who have helped you.

------- •◇• -------

I Have a Bad Manager

In the hustle and bustle of office life, water cooler talks provide a much-needed escape for employees looking to unwind and connect with their colleagues. These informal chats often lead to lively discussions about a figure that stirs a mix of admiration and frustration: their managers.

Suresh, a program manager at a mobile design company, has average performance and finds himself at odds with his manager, whom he doesn't particularly like. Whenever he meets up with friends, the conversation frequently shifts to the complexities of office politics. They share anecdotes about their managers' quirks, decision-making processes, and the unique challenges they each face. Suresh particularly enjoys these moments, as they provide him an opportunity to vent his frustrations about his manager. Each time he shares his frustrations, he feels a sense of relief wash over him, helping him to gain perspective and lighten his emotional load. These discussions not only foster camaraderie but also remind Suresh that he's not alone in navigating the often turbulent waters of workplace dynamics.

His list of complaints is lengthy, but some of the top issues he frequently discusses are:

1. His manager is selfish and focuses on showcasing results to upper management for the sake of his promotion.

2. He suppresses his team, hindering their chances for advancement.

3. He constantly points out areas for improvement as if he himself is perfect.

4. He does not assist in executing projects.

5. He promotes and advances only a select few of his favored (yes-man) employees.

Now, let's delve into the reasons behind Suresh's perception of his manager. Suresh is unaware of several factors that shape this understanding:

1. Jack (Suresh's manager) follows up on progress and keeps management informed to ensure his team receives proper visibility.

2. Jack manages team performance, and the advancement of team members is based on their performance.

3. He collects 360-degree feedback and adds his own insights to provide developmental areas for all team members.

4. Jack believes in granting freedom and ownership to his team members; he isn't a micromanager but is always available to support them.

5. He seeks out opportunities for team members to showcase their accomplishments in front of various teams and management.

Golden words: Often, it's more productive to address challenges with your manager, even if you think he's not effective, rather than turning them into water cooler gossip.

---◇---

I Have a Good Manager

Matt is a dedicated and experienced engineer with over ten years in the industry, working for a leading service company in Bangalore. Known for his sincerity and strong work ethic, he consistently receives high performance ratings. Matt values his positive relationship with his manager, Jack, whom he frequently praises.

Here are some of the key behaviors that Matt appreciates most about Jack and frequently shares with friends:

1. Jack advocates for his team, keeping management informed about their achievements, which enhances the team's reputation.

2. Jack recognizes and rewards the hard work of each team member, ensuring their contributions are acknowledged.

3. Jack provides timely, constructive feedback that significantly contributes to employees' professional growth.

4. Jack offers his team the freedom to manage their work independently, stepping in only when necessary or upon request.

5. Jack personally delivers challenging updates and takes responsibility, while also ensuring team members have opportunities to share positive news.

Now let's look at Matt's working style and see if it has something to with his views on his manager.

1. Matt keeps Jack informed of his progress, especially on tasks that may face challenges or risk falling off track.

2. He puts in his best effort to meet or exceed expectations, and he isn't hesitant to seek help when needed.

3. Matt diligently records all feedback from Jack and always follows up with an actionable plan. If he encounters obstacles, he consults colleagues, mentors, or Jack to stay on track, keeping Jack updated on his progress.

4. He likes taking ownership of his work and enjoys freedom to execute his tasks independently.

5. Matt actively looks for opportunities to talk about his work to various teams, forums and management

The dynamics between a manager and an employee often reflect the employee's behaviors, work ethic, and commitment to growth. A manager's reactions, feedback, and the opportunities they provide are often influenced by the employee's actions and attitude. If you feel your relationship with your manager is off track, it can be helpful to first look inward and consider whether adjusting your own approach could help realign the relationship in a more positive direction.

Golden words: Building the right relationships with your manager and higher-ups is a key factor in achieving career growth.

I Have Bad Employees

Peter, a manager in the design team of a test instrument company, finds himself increasingly frustrated and unmotivated in his role. The challenges he faces with his team have started to affect his overall satisfaction at work, and he often shares his concerns with close friends and colleagues. In these conversations, Peter frequently describes his team's performance and attitude as significant barriers to his productivity.

Some of the key issues he talks are:

1. **Technical Competency:** Peter feels that his team members lack the necessary technical skills required to meet the demands of their roles effectively.

2. **Professional Attitude:** He sees his team members display unprofessional behavior, which impacts both team morale and workflow.

3. **Motivation & Accountability:** According to Peter, there's a general reluctance within the

team to take ownership and work proactively, which limits the team's overall output.

4. **Commitment Concerns:** When Peter attempts to address these issues directly and push for greater accountability, he finds that employees sometimes respond by threatening to leave the company rather than improving the performance.

Peter has developed a habit of discussing his team's performance challenges regularly at work and off work. It's possible he believes that sharing his experiences of managing difficult employees highlights his competency and importance as a manager.

Additionally, he may be seeking empathy from others by projecting his struggles. Of course, there could be various other underlying motivations behind this behaviour.

Now let's look at how Peter's friends can respond when Peter shares his challenges, let's look at some potential responses:

- **Listen without intervention:** Some friends might simply listen, offering a non-judgmental ear without further involvement.

- **Offer advice:** Others may share suggestions to help Peter manage the situation more effectively.

- **Express sympathy:** Certain friends might show empathy, acknowledging Peter's frustrations and offering emotional support.

- **Criticize company policies:** Some could point to organizational policies or senior management as contributing factors, suggesting that Peter's challenges are part of a larger issue.

- **Discuss Peter's situation with others:** A few might share Peter's concerns with others, whether out of worry or as part of casual conversation.

This is a serious concern when a manager, such as Peter, speaks negatively about their team. Such behavior is rarely a good indicator for an organization's health. Here are a few critical questions to consider:

- Is there a chance that Peter's team is aware of his comments about them?

- Could Peter's behavior be contributing to his team's performance challenges?

- Is it possible the team is performing well, but Peter's negativity is affecting his judgment?

- Does this behavior reflect a broader cultural issue within the company, where multiple managers exhibit similar attitudes?

Golden words: A leader's manner of speaking about their team and representing their efforts is a true reflection of their passion for that team.

———————— •◇• ————————

I Have Good Employees

Jack is a manager of a design team, and he exudes happiness and excitement about both his company and his work. He frequently praises his team, emphasizing their ability to excel with minimal guidance. In fact, he often remarks that they are capable of managing their tasks independently, even in the absence him. As a testament to their talent and dedication, Jack's team members are receiving promotions at a faster rate than their peers, reflecting the high level of visibility, trust and respect he has cultivated within the team.

Here are some of the standout qualities Jack highlights about his team:

- My team members are technically proficient and learn quickly.

- They are always polite and considerate, managing responsibilities seamlessly.

- They work so hard that I often have to remind them to take breaks.

- I feel fortunate to have such a dedicated team.

Jack's manager, program managers, and other employees frequently praise Jack's team for their outstanding performance, often citing Jack's commendations as the source of their recognition. Is this a virtuous cycle that is contributing to their success?

Few critical Questions to Consider:

- Is Jack's motivation driving the team to excel technically and acquire new skills?

- Does the team's courteous behavior and sense of accountability reflect Jack's influence?

- Does the team work harder because they see Jack as an integral and valued part of their journey?

- Do team members feel fortunate to have Jack as their manager?

Managers are fundamental pillars of a team and are often a decisive factor in its success or failure. The right manager can inspire a team to push beyond their limits, fostering an environment where growth and development are prioritized. Jack's leadership might be nurturing a team culture of mutual respect, high standards, and commitment to shared goals. When managers lead by example, they empower team members to take ownership and strive for excellence. Selecting leaders like Jack is essential for an organization's long-term success, as they shape not only the team's accomplishments but also the culture of the organization itself.

Golden words: Right managers are the backbone of an organization, providing the strength and support needed for lasting success.

————— •◇• —————

Cunning Manager or Great Manager

Matt is a mechanical engineer at a home appliances company and has been reporting to Jack for the past three years. He believed that he has a good working relationship with his manager. Jack consistently provides Matt with positive feedback and encouragement, and Matt feels satisfied with the work and support he receives.

However, for the past several months, Matt has started feeling confused by his manager's behaviour. Each year, Jack identifies new improvement areas for Matt, acknowledging the progress Matt has made on the previous year's goals but still emphasizing further areas for development.

As this continued into the third year, Matt begins to suspect that Jack may be using praise to get more work out of him without any intention to promote him. Jack's suggestions for improvement always come with reminders about how crucial they are for Matt's career growth and his contributions to the company. However,

Matt started to feel that Jack might be keeping a record of these areas of improvement to potentially prove he's not ready for the promotion or even not fit for the company. Matt grows increasingly convinced that, despite the positive feedback, Jack is subtly building a case to delay his promotion. Over time, Matt's perception of Jack as a cunning manager became more solidified.

Matt didn't want to confront Jack, fearing it might upset him or even cost him his job. While these thoughts weigh on him, Jack's daily encouragements keep him going, though inside, Matt is growing increasingly uncomfortable. Finally he decided to consult his mentor outside the company in a one-on-one meeting. His mentor advised Matt to request a one-on-one with Jack, sending an agenda in advance that clearly states he'd like to discuss his career. He encourages Matt to approach the meeting with a positive mindset, stay calm, and listen closely.

Although Matt isn't entirely sure of a positive outcome, he follows his mentor's advice and sets up the meeting with Jack. Taking a deep breath to steady him, Matt begins the conversation by asking Jack for feedback on his performance and insights into his career path. Jack's response was unexpectedly enthusiastic. "You're doing great, and I'm very proud to have you on the team," he tells Matt. "You've made incredible progress over the last two years, and I'm working on your promotion this year." Jack adds that his own manager sees Matt as a potential future leader. Matt was stunned; he realized that he may have misjudged Jack entirely. To his surprise, Jack reveals that this promotion is actually on a fast track.

Matt felt both relieved and slightly remorseful about his earlier assumptions. He expressed his concern to Jack that he still has areas for improvement. Jack explains that each new level comes with fresh expectations, and consistent growth requires continuously learning skills that foster sustainable progress.

Energized by Jack's feedback, Matt dives back into his work with renewed dedication. He called his mentor to explain the entire discussion and expresses his gratitude for the invaluable advice.

Golden words: Assumptions can be perilous to one's career.

———————— •◇• ————————

Why 1 on 1 With My Manager?

Matt was a Manufacturing Engineer at a leading product company, known for his hard work and sincerity. Reporting to Jack, his manager, Matt shared a good working relationship with him. They interacted regularly in team meetings, project reviews, and occasional one-on-ones when Matt needed to provide project updates. He was genuinely satisfied with his role, his manager, and the company culture.

Recently, however, Matt learned about the importance of mentorship for career development. After speaking with colleagues and gathering insights, he selected a mentor. In their very first meeting, his mentor asked if Matt had regular one-on-one meetings with Jack, specifically for career discussions. Matt realized that while he did have one-on-ones for project updates, he'd never engaged in broader conversations about his career goals or growth with his manager. Until now, he hadn't fully understood the potential impact of these regular one-on-ones on his career progression.

Let's explore how regular one-on-ones with a manager can influence an employee's career in different scenarios:

Scenario 1:

Matt had been working at the same level for the past five years and was eagerly expecting a promotion last year, feeling that his experience and dedication warranted advancement. He trusted that his manager would support his growth. However, during his annual appraisal, Matt received an above-average salary increase but did not get promoted, leaving him disappointed. This pattern repeated again this year, with no change in his role.

After his recent appraisal, Matt couldn't shake the feeling that he was simply there to fulfil tasks, with his contributions overlooked and his value to the team unappreciated. His once-strong motivation faded, replaced by a growing sense of frustration. Questions of self-worth crept in, and he found himself weighing the idea of a job change more seriously. A fresh start, he thought, might be the only way to find the career growth and recognition he was looking for.

Scenario 2:

Two years ago, Matt began regular one-on-one meetings with his manager, Jack, who was approachable and receptive to Matt's career ambitions. In one of these sessions, Matt directly asked Jack what he could do to earn a promotion. Jack, pleased by Matt's initiative and eagerness to grow, mapped out a detailed plan focused on both technical and behavioural growth. He recommended they review Matt's progress each quarter and suggested Matt begin building relationships with other teams who would become his internal clients once he was promoted.

Fueled by Jack's support and belief in his potential, Matt went above and beyond, putting in extra time and energy to not just meet but surpass the expectations set for him. He took on challenging projects, proactively sought feedback, and cultivated a strong network within the company. Jack noticed Matt's consistent dedication and began to speak highly of him to his own manager, sharing examples of Matt's growth and contributions. Both Jack and his manager admired Matt's enthusiasm, resilience, and commitment to personal growth, seeing him as a model of continuous improvement.

After six quarters of unwavering dedication and perseverance, Matt's hard work was rewarded—he received the long-awaited promotion, solidifying his reputation as a rising star in the organization.

Scenario 3:

Matt was proud of his work on the project and felt satisfied with his contributions. However, he couldn't help but feel a bit uneasy about his future, as the technology he was working on was gradually becoming outdated, and he struggled to find time to learn new skills. Matt maintained regular monthly one-on-one meetings with his manager, Jack, where they discussed various aspects of his career and development.

About three months ago, Matt brought up his concern about staying current in a fast-evolving tech landscape. Jack was pleased to see Matt's awareness of industry changes and eagerness to grow. Recognizing Matt's workload, Jack proposed a solution: Matt should focus solely on the development project that leveraged his expertise and pass the support work on to a junior team member who was still learning. This would free up Matt's time to dive into learning the new technology that was becoming increasingly important for the company.

Beyond just encouraging Matt, Jack emphasized how valuable this new technology was to the organization and expressed his excitement about Matt's interest. The conversation left both of them feeling energized and optimistic about Matt's potential for growth.

Golden words: Regular one-on-ones with your manager can be a powerful catalyst for career growth, unlocking new opportunities and insights.

—————— •◇• ——————

Finding a Career Mentor

Matt had over 15 years of experience at a software product company, working as a senior software engineer. He often heard in discussions that having a mentor could be essential for faster career growth, yet he wondered who could be the right mentor for him. With so many potential mentors both within and outside the company, he wasn't sure how to make the best choice.

He had several questions:

- Could the choice of mentor significantly influence his career path?

- Are all mentors equally effective?

- Can any successful employee serve as a good mentor?

- Could an employee who doesn't seem very successful still be a valuable mentor?

To explore these questions, let's examine two distinct scenarios.

Scenario 1:

Matt eventually chose a mentor and explained that he was seeking guidance for career growth. Together, they began holding monthly one-on-one meetings to discuss Matt's progress and goals. In each session, his mentor would ask for project updates, offering guidance to help Matt stay focused and urging him to work diligently to meet his deliverables. Wanting to accelerate his career growth, the mentor even suggested that Matt consider putting in extra hours on weekends and holidays to make faster progress. The mentor reassured Matt that he would be available to assist with any technical challenges that came up, reinforcing the importance of pushing forward with determination.

Matt worked hard and took his mentors help in making progress in project and getting reviewed his project and finding gaps.

Scenario 2:

Matt found a mentor within the company and clarified that his primary goal was career mentorship, specifically aligning his learning with his long-term career path. In their first meeting, his mentor set clear expectations, explaining that he would ask questions about Matt's past and current projects to help refine his career and learning strategy. However, he made it clear that he wouldn't be involved in project reviews or tracking deliverables. For project-specific guidance, he encouraged Matt to consult his project manager and direct supervisor.

The mentor advised Matt to write down his career goals and identify any challenges he faced, suggesting he break these goals into smaller, achievable targets. Together, they developed a strategy and a system to track Matt's progress, enabling him to measure growth and stay motivated as he worked toward his goals.

Different mentors have varied approaches and styles, making them suitable for different needs and objectives. Finding a mentor who aligns well with one's specific goals is crucial to success. Attending trainings on how to identify the right mentor and how to be an effective mentee can be highly beneficial before beginning the mentor search process. Taking mentorship seriously is essential, as it can have a lasting impact on one's career trajectory and personal growth.

Golden words: Good mentors can help shape your career in profound ways, while the absence of guidance or the wrong mentorship can lead to missed opportunities and setbacks.

———————— •◇• ————————

How Many Mentors?

Matt worked as a researcher at an electric vehicle design company, where his manager often emphasized the importance of mentorship in various meetings. Inspired by his manager, Matt wanted to take advantage of having mentors to advance his career. He began actively searching for the right mentors both within and outside the company. While he identified several potential mentors, he was uncertain about asking all of them to take on that role. He had many questions swirling in his mind:

1. Is having more mentors necessarily better?

2. Is there a recommended number of mentors one should have?

3. Should I approach them in a series, one after another?

4. How do I determine how many mentors I should have?

Let's explore some scenarios to address Matt's questions.

Scenario 1:

Matt was thrilled to have found multiple potential mentors willing to help him. He reached out to six of them and began one-on-one meetings with each. However, after a few months, he realized that coordinating meetings with all six was consuming too much of his time. Each mentor offered various suggestions and expected him to take action, which became overwhelming. With advice pouring in from six different sources, Matt struggled to keep track of everything and felt inadequate during each meeting. Gradually, his mentors lost interest; some even expressed that they could no longer continue due to their own busy schedules. This left all the mentors with a negative impression of Matt. Disheartened, Matt began to question the value of mentorship, feeling that its importance had been overstated, as he gained little benefit from having multiple mentors.

Scenario 2:

After consulting with several potential mentors, Matt decided to work with one of the mentors from his company and another from outside. He reasoned that the internal mentor would provide insights into the company culture, while the external mentor would offer a broader industry perspective. By optimizing the frequency of his meetings to fit around his regular responsibilities, Matt found a sustainable schedule: he met with his internal mentor every six weeks and his external mentor every eight weeks. This approach prevented meetings from becoming overwhelming.

Matt was able to take actionable steps based on the advice from both mentors, benefiting from their distinct viewpoints. His external mentor significantly contributed to his professional growth, and both mentors were impressed with his progress.

This strategy proved effective for Matt and his mentors, as it allowed him to invest less time in meetings while still receiving valuable guidance.

Golden words: Strategically choosing the right mentors helps achieve both short- and long-term goals.

———————— •◇• ————————

Day-18

Duration of a Mentorship

A few months ago, Matt was promoted to a managerial role at a multinational pharmaceutical company. Serious about advancing his career, he recognized that this new position would require him to develop new skills, so he began searching for a mentor.

After a few weeks, Matt found a mentor within his company and began regular sessions with her. In a one-on-one meeting with his manager, Matt shared that he had approached Mahi, a respected employee in a different department, to be his mentor and had already started working with her. Pleased with Matt's proactive approach to learning, his manager asked if he had discussed both his goals and the expected duration of the mentorship with Mahi. While Matt had set clear goals, he hadn't considered the importance of defining a timeframe.

Let's look at some scenarios that highlight why setting duration is as crucial as setting goals.

Scenario 1:

Matt started monthly sessions with Mahi but realized after three meetings that her suggestions didn't quite align with his needs. Mahi's approach was different from what worked in his department, making it difficult for Matt to apply her advice. Concerned that ending the mentorship might offend Mahi—a senior member of the organization—Matt felt stuck. He continued the sessions, even though he wasn't benefiting, and gradually began to doubt the value of mentorship itself, wondering if it could truly help anyone.

Scenario 2:

At the beginning of their mentorship, Matt shared his goals with Mahi and asked if she could mentor him for an initial six-month period. After three sessions, he realized that her approach didn't align well with his team's practices. In their sixth session, Matt thanked Mahi for her guidance, mentioned how he appreciated her time, and asked if she'd be open to occasional future guidance if needed. With a set timeframe, both Matt and Mahi concluded the mentorship on positive terms.

Scenario 3:

As with the previous scenario, Matt began his mentorship with Mahi by discussing his goals and requesting a six-month engagement. Over the next three months, he found Mahi's advice incredibly valuable, helping him clarify his thinking and turn ideas into actionable steps. In their fourth one-on-one, Matt shared how impactful her mentorship had been and asked if she would be willing to extend the mentorship for another six months. Mahi agreed, and they happily continued working together with renewed purpose.

Golden words: Setting the mentorship duration at the outset is crucial, as a mentor who suits one individual may not be right for another.

————— •◇• —————

Closing a Successful Mentorship

Matt is a dedicated and sincere software developer who takes his career seriously. He invests significant effort to steer it in the right direction, understanding that guidance can be crucial. Recognizing the value of mentorship, Matt found a mentor and enjoyed a productive mentoring experience. However, he wasn't entirely sure when or how to bring this mentorship engagement to a close.

Setting clear goals and defining a timeframe at the outset of any mentorship is essential. Not every mentor will be the perfect fit, so beginning with a shorter commitment—such as six months—can be beneficial. Every mentorship, whether successful or not, must eventually conclude. While there are rare cases where mentorships span decades, such as 20-30 years, these are exceptional rather than typical.

To understand the importance of properly concluding a mentorship, let's consider different scenarios:

Matt began his career mentorship with Mahi, a highly successful senior employee at his company, two years ago. Right from the start, Matt set clear goals, and their mentorship was productive, allowing him to achieve his targeted objectives. With a recent promotion, Matt now aims to develop new skills, so he's looking to engage a mentor more suited to his evolving role.

Scenario 1:

Throughout their mentorship, Matt held monthly one-on-one meetings with Mahi, along with ad hoc discussions as needed. When he decided to move on, he began by canceling regular meetings and gradually reduced the frequency of their interactions. However, he felt increasingly uncomfortable about telling Mahi that he no longer wished to continue their mentorship. He worried that Mahi might not react well to him seeking a new mentor, potentially even feeling hurt by the decision.

As a result, Matt began to avoid Mahi, which led to discomfort on both sides. Mahi noticed the change and felt uncertain about Matt's behaviour, which strained their previously positive rapport.

Scenario 2:

Matt expressed to Mahi how deeply grateful he was for her mentorship, emphasizing how her guidance had been instrumental not only in his recent promotion but also in setting a clear and promising path for his career. He shared that her support had boosted his confidence in navigating complex challenges and helped him reach new milestones. Additionally, he mentioned that he would benefit from one or two more sessions with her as he transitioned into his new role. For their final meeting, Matt made special preparations:

- He wrote a heartfelt, handwritten letter to thank Mahi, detailing the ways her mentorship had guided him and contributed to his growth.

- Knowing Mahi had a fondness for quality pens, Matt gifted her well-crafted pen, noting in his letter that it symbolized the impact she'd had on his career.

- He prepared a presentation highlighting some of Mahi's key advice, the challenges she helped him overcome, and the accomplishments that resulted from their work together.

After expressing his heartfelt gratitude, Matt shared his hope that Mahi would be available for occasional guidance in the future as he continued to grow in his career. He emphasized how much he valued her insights and mentorship and would appreciate her support if new challenges arose. Both Matt and Mahi felt satisfied with this positive closure, and Mahi reassured him that he could always reach out if he needed help going forward.

Golden words: Always keep the door open for future engagements as you conclude a mentorship.

———————— •◇• ————————

Day-20

Data Magic in Meetings

Matt is a dedicated software engineer with over ten years of experience at his company. Known for his hard work and commitment, he has earned recognition as a high-potential employee, consistently receiving exceptional ratings for his knowledge and performance. Despite several colleagues exhibiting similar dedication and expertise, Matt's ratings consistently surpass theirs. This disparity has led to surprise and speculation among his peers, with some questioning whether he enjoys favouritism from management.

Let's explore the actions that might contribute to Matt's superior ratings compared to his colleagues:

- **Proactive Monitoring:** Matt regularly reviews his project schedules, noting any changes to key milestones.

- **Engagement with Leadership:** He takes the initiative to discuss milestone changes with project managers, architects, and his direct manager to understand the underlying reasons.

- **Active Participation:** In project meetings, Matt attentively listens for risks and mitigation strategies employed by other teams, enhancing his understanding of the broader project landscape.

- **Building Networks:** He keeps a detailed record of key contacts, not only for his projects but also for two to three additional projects involving his teammates.

- **Documentation:** Matt diligently notes down important points from his observations and discussions.

Let's examine a few scenarios to understand how Matt's image is being shaped and whether it relates to the actions he is taking.

Scenario 1:

During a project review attended by several engineers and senior leaders, a significant change in a milestone was highlighted. While other engineers hesitated, unsure of the details, Matt confidently provided the rationale behind the change. When asked about key contacts in another group, it was Matt who had the right data. This confident display of knowledge positioned Matt distinctly in the eyes of senior leadership compared to his peers.

Scenario 2:

One day, while returning from lunch, Matt stepped into the elevator and found himself alongside his division director. After exchanging a few pleasantries, the director inquired about the status of the upcoming beta release. Matt explained candidly that the release was currently delayed due to a bug recently identified by the testing group. The director thanked him for the update and mentioned he would reach out to the testing team's manager to see if they could help speed up the resolution process.

Few points to think

Could it be that Matt's proactive communication strategies distinguish him from his colleagues?

Do these seemingly straightforward actions play a significant role in shaping how he is perceived by leadership, ultimately contributing to his high performance ratings?

Golden words: Embrace your role and company culture, and aim to exceed expectations. Even an extra 15 minutes a day of consistent effort can lead to meaningful differentiation.

Data Blunder...

In the same role, people can interact differently and interpret situations in unique ways. While everyone believes they are doing well, career progress varies from person to person. Let's explore how interactions and responses to various situations can influence career advancement through Matt's story. For the past six years, Matt has been a dedicated and hardworking employee in supply chain management, specializing in aluminium components for newly launched products.

Let's examine Matt's approach to his environment in two different scenarios to see if it might be affecting his career advancement.

Scenario 1:

Matt was known for his diligence and focus, consistently dedicating himself to his specific responsibilities. He rarely engaged in activities outside his immediate tasks, often skipping meetings that weren't directly relevant to his projects or that didn't require his input. This intense focus even led him to miss several all-staff meetings.

During one of Matt's regular project meetings, his manager's manager joined and asked if all suppliers had been finalized for the project. Since the project manager was absent, he directed the question to Matt, who responded that he didn't have that information. Another day, while heading to his desk, Matt was casually approached by a senior manager who asked, "Hey Matt, how are you? I heard copper prices are rising. Do you know what's happening with that?" Matt, as usual, replied, "Sorry, I'm not aware."

Later, in a feedback session with other managers, Matt's supervisor gathered input on his team. The responses about Matt were mixed: "Matt is good, but he doesn't seem fully engaged," said one manager. Another remarked, "I haven't had many interactions with him." Some feedback suggested that, although he had a reputation as a solid worker, limited interactions with him didn't always leave a positive impression.

Despite his dedication and productivity, Matt's career progression has been noticeably slow.

Scenario 2:

Matt was known for his diligence and focus, consistently dedicating himself to his responsibilities. He made it a point to attend project meetings or, when unable to do so, to review the meeting minutes. During lunch and tea breaks, he was eager to learn about other materials and projects, often engaging in conversations to stay informed. Additionally, he regularly attended his manager's staff meetings, where he actively asked questions and participated in discussions.

During a project meeting, Matt's manager's manager inquired whether all the suppliers had been finalized for the project. With the project manager absent, he turned to Matt for an update. Matt confidently responded, "Yes, all suppliers were finalized two days ago, and the project manager plans to send out the report by the end of this week." The manager expressed his appreciation, saying, "Very good! A big thank you to the team for this achievement."

On another occasion, as Matt was walking toward his desk, a senior manager greeted him and asked, "Hey Matt, how are you? I heard the cost of copper parts is going up. Do you know what's happening?" Matt replied, "Yes, the project manager mentioned it's due to geopolitical reasons. He's working with the team to explore vendors and partners in another country." The senior manager was pleased with this quick update, responding, "Thanks, Matt! I'll talk to the project manager in the next 2-3 days to get further details for our product."

Later, when Matt's manager collected feedback from other managers about his team members. Most responses about Matt were positive, with comments like, "Matt is intelligent and stays up to date," and "I haven't interacted with him much, but in the few small interactions I've had, he seems to be good".

Matt was making good career advancements.

Golden words: Awareness of your surroundings is a powerful asset for your career, easily cultivated through consistent mindfulness and engagement.

Day-22

Lunch That Leads to Success

Matt was a talented software engineer renowned for his exceptional skills and efficiency, often completing projects faster than his peers. While he shared the hardworking and intelligent traits of many others in the company, Matt had a distinct advantage: a vast network of connections across various departments and domains.

This network was a key factor in the swift progress of his work. His colleagues often marvelled at how someone so dedicated to his responsibilities could get time to cultivate such a wide and robust network.

What many of his peers overlooked, however, was how Matt utilized his lunchtime.

Let's explore how Matt utilized his lunchtimes to consciously foster connections and enhance his professional network.

1. After a meeting with hardware engineers, Matt introduced himself to an engineer he had met for the first time. During their conversation, the engineer mentioned he was from Shimoga

in Karnataka. Matt replied, "I've heard a lot about Shimoga; could you tell me more about it sometime?" The engineer agreed, and Matt proposed they meet for lunch the following day to discuss Shimoga. Their lunch turned into a rich exchange, allowing Matt to learn a great deal about the region.

2. When Matt encountered a bug in his code, a colleague suggested he seek help from an expert in another team. After a productive meeting with the expert, Matt received valuable insights and advice. The expert also recommended a book to help improve Matt's skills. Curious, Matt asked, "Do you read these kinds of books regularly?" The expert responded, "Oh yes, I have many of them." Seizing the opportunity, Matt suggested they have lunch together later that week so he could learn more about the books that could benefit him. Two days later, they enjoyed lunch together, during which the expert shared several of his book recommendations.

3. Although Matt typically brought his lunch from home, he still enjoyed visiting the café to have lunch with friends. One day when he went to cafe he noticed an employee sitting alone. Matt approached him and asked if he could share the table. It turned out the employee was from the finance department and had come from another site for work. They talked about their

experiences, families, hometowns, schooling, and more, exchanging contact information. Just like that, Matt expanded his network to include a friend in finance.

4. Matt was also a skilled trainer who occasionally conducted internal training sessions on software skills. After one such session, a few younger employees had numerous questions. While he answered many, he needed to rush to another meeting. Recognizing their eagerness to learn, he suggested they have lunch together to discuss their questions in more depth. A week later, Matt met for lunch with four of the employees from his training session, allowing for an engaging and informative conversation.

Through these intentional lunchtime interactions, Matt not only expanded his knowledge but also strengthened his professional network, demonstrating the power of engagement in fostering relationships and personal growth.

Golden words: Proper utilization of time can yield significant returns in the long term.

Tea to Shine

Matt, a senior software engineer at a large multinational corporation, has been working on AI-driven projects. Known for his well-rounded approach, he balances his professional duties with a strong commitment to personal development and health. While he's an above-average employee, Matt's growth trajectory has outpaced that of his peers—even those who might be putting in longer hours. His reputation is one of a well-rounded, proactive team player who builds meaningful professional connections, stays attuned to industry trends, and consistently updates his knowledge on emerging technologies.

But what truly drives Matt's success? Is it simply a stroke of luck that he landed in an excellent team with a supportive manager invested in his career growth, or are Matt's achievements the result of deliberate, focused efforts?

Let's take a closer look at some of the unique strategies that set Matt apart, positioning him ahead of peers who appear to be working harder but seeing less progress.

On most days, Matt takes two tea breaks, using these moments as opportunities to reconnect with colleagues he hasn't spoken to in a while. He often reaches out with a simple message, noting it's been some time since they last caught up, and asks if they'd like to meet over tea. Occasionally, he even adjusts his tea break to fit the availability of the colleague he's hoping to meet. Recognizing that everyone has unique interests, Matt listens attentively and engages thoughtfully, asking questions to understand their perspectives. If he finds their conversation intriguing or educational, he'll often suggest meeting again over tea the following day. Through these interactions, Matt continually expands his knowledge—not only in technology but also in areas like company insights, sports, politics, and more.

These conversations often reveal challenges other teams are facing, and Matt actively looks for ways to assist. When he has relevant expertise, he offers solutions, and if not, he connects them with others who might be able to help. Sometimes, simply being a compassionate listener is all that's needed. He's also open to sharing his own technical hurdles, fostering a culture of mutual support.

When Matt encounters something new he wants to learn, he doesn't hesitate to reach out. A typical approach might be, "I have a question about XXXX technology—could you help me?" If that person doesn't have the expertise, he'll politely ask for an introduction to someone who does. Matt's determination to gain knowledge keeps him asking until he finds the answers he's looking for, ensuring he's always growing and staying informed.

Over the past year, Matt has engaged in tea conversations with a wide variety of colleagues, building connections across multiple levels and departments within the organization. He's sat down with his immediate teammates, engineers from other groups, his manager and even his manager's manager, as well as program managers, HR representatives, hardware engineers, and members of the operations management team. Through these conversations, Matt has created a broad network of connections that enrich his understanding of the company's inner workings and the diverse perspectives of those who keep it running.

Could Matt's habit of regular tea conversations be the secret behind his strong reputation, great network, and depth of knowledge? Is it simply a casual break, or is it a powerful strategy that fuels his professional success? These moments he spends connecting with others—could they be the key differentiator setting him apart in his career?

Golden words: Time invested intelligently and thoughtfully is the currency of progress; every minute spent with purpose and wisdom inches you closer to your goals.

————————•◇•————————

Weekends to Wealth

Matt is highly focused on advancing his career and consistently invests time in upskilling himself. With over five years of experience under his belt, he's taken a different approach than many of his friends and colleagues, who are primarily focused on switching jobs to secure salary hikes. Instead, Matt remains committed to building a strong career foundation and enhancing his skill set, prioritizing long-term growth over immediate financial gain.

When a friend asked him about his calm attitude and lack of urgency to seek a higher-paying job, Matt shared a few of his guiding principles:

1. He's committed to growing within his current company and feels that he's making solid progress where he is.

2. Job-hopping, he believes, can bring unnecessary stress, and relocating for a new role might lead to additional expenses that outweigh the immediate financial gain.

3. Every weekend, he spends 3-4 hours studying investment strategies and connecting with others who share similar interests. For the past three years, he has been investing in equities and other diversified assets, achieving an impressive annual growth rate of 18%. With a clear investment roadmap, Matt has mapped out when he plans to allocate funds to assets like gold and real estate, building toward a long-term vision of financial stability. Confident in his strategy, he anticipates that in the next 5-10 years, he will have not only a fulfilling career but also a strong foundation of wealth and stability.

Hearing this, Matt's friend became even more curious and asked him to share more details about his typical weekend routine. Matt explained:

"I structure about 12-14 hours of my weekend, leaving the rest unplanned. Here's how it typically breaks down:

- **3-4 hours** on investments: meeting with friends who have similar financial goals, attending trainings or seminars, reading, and researching various investment options.

- **2-3 hours** spent on one of the meals—lunch or dinner—with colleagues or friends, which helps maintain my personal network.

- **4 hours** focused on up skilling for my current role, ensuring I stay updated in this fast-paced field.

- **2 hours** dedicated to exercise, whether it's hitting the gym, going for a hike, or doing other physical activities.

- **1 hour** on Sundays to review emails and plan for the upcoming week.

The rest of the time remains unplanned and varies depending on the week. Sometimes, it goes toward extra sleep, family time, watching movie, personal errands like banking, or catching up on any remaining office tasks."

Could Matt's balanced weekend routine be the key to his success? Does the way he invests in his career, finances, and personal well-being create a steady rhythm that propels him forward—without the stress or pressure of constantly chasing the next goal? What if this careful balance is the secret to staying ahead while maintaining a sense of calm and control?

Golden words: It takes time and consistent effort to build wealth, but taking care of it can pave the way for growth in many aspects of life.

———————— •◇• ————————

Complacency...a Career Trap!

Suresh is a mechanical design engineer who has dedicated over eight years of his career to his current company. This is the second company in his professional journey, having joined after 7-month tenure at his previous workplace.

During his initial years, he invested significant time in comprehensive training to master the required skills, equipping himself with the expertise needed for success. After completing this essential training phase, he transitioned to consistent project work within his area of specialization, where he has continued to grow and apply his skills.

In his personal life, Suresh found a satisfying balance, enjoying his job and personal time. His happiness in his current role allowed him to spend his evenings and weekends on various leisure activities—whether going out with friends, catching the latest movies, or simply unwinding after a productive week. His life was a steady, fulfilling mix of professional and personal satisfaction.

However, a shift in the market landscape brought unexpected changes. His company was acquired by a larger organization with a new vision and strategy. The new management redefined the company's direction and began to reshape its project portfolio, driven primarily by the value of the intellectual property (IP) his company possessed. Their primary goal was to leverage this IP to strengthen their position against rapidly growing competitors. As part of this strategic pivot, the decision was made to close the division where Suresh had been working for years, putting his role in jeopardy.

With the closure of his division, many of Suresh's colleagues faced a similar predicament. Some were able to find alternative positions within the company's remaining divisions, allowing them to continue their work in new areas. Others decided to take this as an opportunity to move on, accepting attractive offers from other companies with substantial salary increases.

Suresh faced significant challenges in securing a new job, both within his current company and in the external job market. As he explored options, he reached out to some of his friends to understand how they managed to successfully land new roles. During these conversations, he was surprised to learn about the proactive steps his peers had taken to stay relevant in a rapidly evolving job landscape. Many of them had embraced continuous learning, actively acquiring the latest skills and knowledge required in the field. They explained that they had been up skilling themselves in cutting-edge technologies, including those widely used by competitors in the industry.

In addition to technical skills, they had also invested time in building strong professional networks, recognizing the importance of connections in finding new opportunities. Suresh came to a sobering realization: unlike his peers, he had not kept up with recent advancements. He had been relying on the skills he gained during the early years of his career, without making efforts to expand his expertise or adapt to the changing demands of his industry.

Caught unprepared, Suresh found himself in a difficult situation. With limited options, he had to accept a position that offered a significantly lower salary and a less prestigious role than he had previously held.

A few thought-provoking questions to reflect on:

Did Suresh's comfort with his routine ultimately lead to his unpreparedness for change? Could he have better anticipated the evolving demands of his field? While enjoying his evenings and weekends was certainly rewarding, might he have also used some of that time to invest in personal growth? Could a balance between relaxation and skill development have better equipped him to face unexpected shifts in his career?

Golden words: Complacency is a career killer; it lulls you into mediocrity, halting your growth and potential.

Fire Brand Employee!

Matt, a talented mechanical design engineer and lead at his company, recently completed a project that, while relatively straightforward, required exceptional precision and meticulous attention to detail. Though it was considered a moderate priority within the company, Matt approached it with a strong sense of responsibility and a desire to add value. As the project advanced, he diligently documented every new step, enhancement, and improvement introduced by him and his team, meticulously compiling these insights into a detailed and comprehensive record. Recognizing the importance of knowledge-sharing, he proactively shared this list with wider team, hoping it might serve as a valuable resource for future projects or as a reference for his colleagues.

In addition, Matt went a step further to visually document the project by taking photos that showcased each stage of progress. He then posted these images on the company's internal portal, offering others a clear, visual understanding of the work that had been done. His initiative not only highlighted his own contributions but also fostered a sense of transparency and teamwork within the department.

Throughout the duration of the project, Matt remained actively engaged. He participated fully in every meeting, consistently contributing thoughtful insights and suggestions. His proactive involvement was well-noted, as he demonstrated his commitment to the project and his enthusiasm for continuous improvement.

After some time, Matt was entrusted with a new assignment, which was notably more complex and challenging than his previous projects. It quickly became clear to him that this project held significant importance to the company's strategic goals, and he understood the impact of project could have on the organization's success. As he tackled the new challenges, Matt maintained open lines of communication with his management team, regularly updating them on any obstacles encountered and discussing the critical nature of the project and progress.

Each time a milestone was achieved, Matt ensured that he informed his superiors in a timely, clear, and professional manner, reinforcing his reliability and commitment to transparency. His diligence in communicating progress not only kept his management in the loop but also demonstrated his understanding of the project's value to the company.

Matt took a thoughtful and strategic approach to communicating his progress and achievements.

He was mindful to present his updates in a way that was professional and understated, ensuring that his communication never appeared boastful or self-serving. Rather than seeking personal recognition, his goal was to highlight the tangible value his work brought to the team and the organization as a whole. By framing his contributions in this way, he subtly reinforced how his efforts were aligned with the company's objectives and how his proactive problem-solving could benefit others.

This considerate approach to self-presentation allowed Matt to gain increased visibility within the company. His work became more widely recognized not just as individual achievements, but as meaningful contributions to the team's success. In doing so, he strengthened his reputation as a reliable and impactful team member. Over time, his superiors and colleagues came to view him as a vital contributor to the organization, appreciating his collaborative spirit, dedication, and professional integrity. Matt's balanced communication style helped him establish a lasting presence within the company, positioning him as an emerging leader and a trusted member of the team.

Golden words: Personal branding plays a crucial role in career progression, as it helps individuals distinguish themselves, showcase their unique skills, and build a reputation that opens doors to new opportunities.

Fail to Fit!

Every company operates much like a living organism, each with its own unique culture, values, and ways of working. These differences shape the work environment, expectations, and even the daily rhythm of employees' lives.

Suresh had been working at a large, established organization for over seven years. He was happy there and felt he was making steady career progress. However, an exciting opportunity arose for him to join a much smaller company, offering him a higher position and a significant salary increase. After careful consideration, Suresh decided to make the leap and accepted the new role.

Upon joining the new company, Suresh participated in an employee induction program, which gave him a general overview of the company's operations and expectations. He then began working with his assigned team, diving into his new responsibilities.

One day, Suresh's friend, whose office was nearby, dropped by to visit. Suresh took a quick break and joined his friend at a nearby café for a coffee, expecting to be back at his desk shortly. About fifteen minutes into their conversation, Suresh's phone rang—it was his manager. The manager asked why he wasn't present at a meeting. Surprised, Suresh explained that he hadn't seen any meeting invite yet. His manager replied that he'd sent it out thirty minutes earlier, but Suresh hadn't noticed since he'd been busy with his tasks before stepping out to meet his friend. Later, in a one-on-one, his manager said that meeting friends is fine, but meetings should not be missed.

As Suresh settled into his role, he observed that the company's work culture was quite different from what he was accustomed to.

The norm in this new workplace was for employees to put in extended hours—typically around 10 to 11 hours daily—and to come into the office on most weekends. One evening, as Suresh was about to head home after a full day's work, one of his team leaders approached him, inviting him to join the team at the café. They were planning to have a meal together before staying late to work on a project. This expectation of longer hours and the tendency for spontaneous after-hours gatherings was a notable shift from Suresh's previous work environment.

Suresh found it challenging to adjust to the new company's culture and working style. Unlike his previous organization, where structured processes and clear guidelines were the norm, this smaller company operated with a more ad-hoc approach. Decisions were often made on the fly, with team leaders and managers having the final say, leaving little room for structured planning. Suresh found himself caught off guard by last-minute meetings, changing priorities, and spontaneous requests, which created a work environment that felt unpredictable and, at times, chaotic.

In his previous company, processes were well-defined, and the company had policies that were notably employee-friendly. Each employee had a good level of control over their workday, planning their tasks according to the demands of their projects. Meetings were typically scheduled well in advance, allowing Suresh to organize his day efficiently and maintain a good work-life balance. The structured environment allowed him to focus on his work without the stress of constantly shifting expectations.

After six months of trying to adapt, Suresh found that his discomfort and unease only continued to grow. The lack of structure, combined with the expectation of long hours and weekend work, weighed heavily on him.

Realizing that he thrived in a more process-driven, organized setting, Suresh ultimately decided to leave. He accepted a position with another large organization known for its strong processes and employee-cantered policies, similar to the environment he had previously enjoyed.

Golden words: Every company has its own culture, work style, and ways of recognizing employees. Understanding and adapting to these differences quickly is key to building a successful career.

———————— •◇• ————————

Meeting Notes... a Secret Weapon!

Taking notes during meetings is often overlooked by employees and sometimes even seen as outdated. However, keeping a notebook and jotting down key points is a powerful habit with many hidden benefits that can support career growth and improve one's image.

Note-taking keeps you engaged and focused, minimizing distractions and keeping wandering thoughts in check. It also helps capture important details like new terms, technologies, names of people, or project titles that come up during discussions—details that can easily slip from memory afterward. By actively recording these points, you create a personal reference that can prove invaluable for follow-up actions and for showing attention to detail.

Suresh experienced firsthand the drawbacks of not taking notes. In a one-on-one meeting, his manager asked if he had connected with the project leader for Project Tiger, a task they had previously discussed. Suresh, unfortunately, had forgotten both the action item and the project leader's name. Embarrassed, he had to ask his manager for the name again. In another meeting, his manager inquired about the purchase order amount for workstations they'd discussed earlier. Suresh hesitated, unsure if it was $10,000 or $15,000, which made him appear uncertain and unprepared.

While Suresh believed he was performing well, he was unaware that his manager was beginning to view him as a passive listener, somewhat careless, and unreliable with details. This perception, shaped by his lack of preparation and forgetfulness, was gradually impacting his professional image.

Suresh's peer, Matt, who also reports to the same manager, has developed the habit of carrying a notebook and making concise notes for each meeting. He's organized his notebook into five distinct sections: 1) Staff and Team, 2) Project A, 3) Project B, 4) Learning and Other Notes, and 5) One-on-Ones. For every entry, Matt includes the date and the name of the meeting in the relevant section, creating an easy-to-navigate system.

Throughout the day, Matt routinely glances at his notebook to remind himself of action items or pending follow-up tasks, which helps him stay organized and on top of his responsibilities. His note-taking habit allows him to quickly find details in meetings, even if he doesn't remember them right away.

Two weeks ago, in a staff meeting, Matt's manager asked if he could recall the key points they had discussed and planned for the team's upcoming customer demo event. Matt responded confidently, 'Sure.' As he began speaking, he quickly found his notes in his diary, seamlessly covering each point with clarity and precision.

This method allows him to provide accurate information almost immediately without delay.

Matt's approach is also less distracting in meetings compared to opening a laptop to search for data, which can draw attention and break the flow of conversation. His simple yet structured approach keeps him both prepared and responsive, enhancing his ability to contribute seamlessly during discussions. By relying on his organized notebook, Matt projects a focused and attentive demeanour that reflects his commitment to efficiency and readiness.

Despite having similar knowledge and performance in project execution as Suresh, Matt's manager is forming a notably positive impression of him. Matt's habit of note-taking and his quick responses in meetings paint him as an active listener, proactive, and a smart worker. This image of being highly organized and attentive is steadily enhancing Matt's professional reputation.

Golden words: Small habits, when nurtured consistently, lay the foundation for extraordinary achievements in your career. It's the seemingly insignificant actions that, over time, create the most profound impact.

Day-29

Dress to Fit!

Every company operates with a set of unwritten rules that guide behaviour, even though they may not be explicitly stated in any policy document. One of the most common unwritten rules is employee dress code. While many companies may have general guidelines about formal or business-casual attire, employees often pick up on the subtle cues about what is acceptable based on how their colleagues and leaders dress.

For example, in some workplaces, "casual Fridays" might mean jeans and a T-shirt, while in others, it might mean khakis and a polo shirt. Another unwritten rule might be how employees communicate with leadership—some environments encourage casual, open conversations, while others expect more formal, hierarchical interactions.

Similarly, when it comes to taking breaks or leaving the office, there may be a spoken rule about working hours, but employees learn the real expectations by observing when most people come in or leave.

Let's look into some examples on how dress can potentially impact our career progression:

Suresh's story:

Suresh was thrilled to start his new role at a marketing firm, eager to make a positive first impression. In preparation, he'd carefully reviewed the employee handbook, which mentioned a 'business casual' dress code. Wanting to be seen as polished and professional, he decided to wear a sharp, tailored suit on his first day, confident that this would signal his commitment to the job.

When he arrived, however, he quickly noticed a stark contrast between his attire and that of his colleagues. Many were dressed in jeans, polos, and comfortable sneakers, exuding a relaxed, approachable vibe.

Suresh began to feel somewhat out of place, but he decided to stick to his formal wardrobe, believing it would underscore his dedication and professionalism.

As the weeks went by, though, Suresh began to sense an unintended consequence. Despite his diligence and consistent hard work, he noticed a growing sense of isolation. In team meetings and casual office conversations, his colleagues seemed at ease with one another, joking and chatting freely, while he felt like an outsider in these interactions.

Matt's story:

Matt joined a tech start-up known for its flexible work culture. The company had no formal dress code, and Matt noticed during his interview that everyone wore casual clothes—T-shirts, jeans, and even hoodies. Wanting to fit in, he mirrored their style from day one.

This choice paid off. Matt found that because he blended into the company culture visually, it was easier for him to strike up casual conversations with his peers. He was quickly included in brainstorming sessions, and team leads sought his input more often. Without any formal barriers, his colleagues felt comfortable around him, which made collaboration smoother.

Both above stories highlight how something as simple as dress code, even when it's not formally enforced, can play a significant role in an employee's ability to fit in and thrive within a company. By reading the unsaid rules of how to dress and adjusting accordingly, Matt was able to fit seamlessly into the culture, which accelerated his integration into the team and helped him make faster progress in his role.

Golden words: Success often depends on mastering the unsaid rules that unlock opportunity and connection.

Day-30

Energy to Move Faster!

In every office, it's common to see some employees who look very active and energetic, while others seem relatively dull and passive.

Ever wondered if this could be linked to career progression?

Generally, who appear energetic tend to stand out; they often come across as more engaged, motivated, and ready to tackle new challenges. This vibrant presence not only influences how they are perceived by colleagues and supervisors but also impacts their own performance—boosting productivity, creativity, and resilience under pressure. On the other hand, employees who seem passive or disengaged may struggle to command the same attention or opportunities.

Suresh's story

Suresh was often seen as a capable but passive employee. He did his work but rarely showed much enthusiasm or energy, even when things were going smoothly. When a major client requested last-minute changes to a project, Suresh's team was thrown into chaos.

His manager, Jack, called him in to discuss the situation. "Suresh, we need to revise the entire proposal by the end of the day. Can you take the lead on this?" jack asked.

Suresh sighed heavily, looking overwhelmed. "I'll try, but it's going to be difficult with all the other work I have," he said in a low, unenthusiastic tone. Instead of taking initiative, Suresh simply followed his usual routine, dragging his feet and working through the tasks without a sense of urgency or direction.

His lack of energy not only stifled his own productivity but also drained his team's morale, as they were inevitably affected by his sluggish demeanor.

When the deadline approached, the project was only partially done, forcing Jack to step in and make last-minute corrections herself. Although the project was delivered, it wasn't the quality the client expected, and Jack had to apologize for the delays. Senior management wasn't pleased either.

Matt's story

Matt was known around the office for his high energy and positive attitude, even during tough situations. His workday was filled with challenges—tight deadlines, a heavy workload, and unexpected problems—but Matt maintained an active, energetic posture throughout.

Even when his team's project hit a roadblock due to a sudden change in client requirements, Matt didn't flinch. He gathered his team for a quick brainstorming session, looking for solutions instead of dwelling on the issue.

One day, Matt's manager, Jack, called him in to discuss an urgent project that was falling behind. The team was already stretched thin, and Jack needed someone to step up and take charge. "Matt, I know this is a tough ask with everything else going on, but could you lead this effort? We need it done by the end of the week," he said, glancing at his already busy schedule.

Matt nodded confidently, saying, "I'll get it done. Let me delegate some tasks to the team, and I'll focus on driving this forward."

He quickly broke the project into manageable parts, distributing responsibilities among his teammates, and led the effort with his usual energetic approach.

His willingness to take charge and stay upbeat impressed Jack.

Jack mentioned Matt's leadership to the senior management team in a meeting later that week.

Golden words: The energy you bring to tasks and the workplace shapes the trajectory of your career.

Show It!

Many employees understand the importance of demonstrating activeness and energy at work, but they often fear being perceived negatively. They worry that managers might think their focus is lacking or that they won't be seen as sincere workers. Additionally, some simply feel uncertain about how to project that energy effectively. These challenges are common for a significant percentage of employees.

Suresh's story

Suresh had been with the company for five years, and everyone knew him as a reliable, hardworking, and sincere employee. He completed his tasks with precision and often went the extra mile to meet deadlines. However, Suresh was more focused on getting his work done than on how he presented himself. He dressed modestly, steered clear of unnecessary attention, and preferred solitude, trusting that his accomplishments would quietly tell his story.

In meetings, Suresh usually remained quiet unless asked for his input, assuming that staying in the background was better than drawing attention. Though his performance was solid, he never volunteered to lead projects or showcase his ideas proactively. Suresh rarely engaged with senior leadership beyond work matters and didn't make an effort to connect with others on social media.

Over time, Suresh started noticing that opportunities for promotions and project leads were being given to others—colleagues who, in his opinion, weren't outperforming him but were more visible, more vocal, and seemed to have the attention of management. His manager praised his work ethic, but when leadership roles were discussed, Suresh's name never came up. He felt frustrated, seeing people with similar or even lesser performance being promoted while he remained in the same position.

Matt's story

Matt was always a diligent worker, but he realized that simply doing his tasks well wasn't enough if he wanted to stand out. He decided to put conscious effort into projecting energy and enthusiasm at work. He updated his wardrobe to more polished, professional outfits, making sure he looked sharp every day. Matt also started paying attention to his body language—sitting up straight in meetings, smiling, and making direct eye contact with his peers, managers, and senior leaders.

In conversations, Matt adopted a more upbeat tone, actively listening to his colleagues and responding with enthusiasm. During meetings, he made it a point to offer ideas and ask thoughtful questions, showing his engagement. He also began taking more initiative, offering help to other teams when he had some bandwidth, which caught the attention of his manager. On social media, Matt shared relevant industry articles and company achievements, subtly reinforcing his professional brand.

Over time, Matt's proactive behaviour didn't go unnoticed. His managers saw him not just as a hardworking employee, but as someone with leadership potential. His energy and confidence made him stand out in cross-department meetings. When a project lead position opened up, Matt was selected for the role, and colleagues began to look to him for guidance. Senior management soon started discussing him as a future leader within the company.

Golden words: Showing energy and activeness at work is just as crucial as working efficiently—it's the spark that turns competence into leadership potential.

———————— •◇• ————————

Day-32

The Power of Questions to Grow

Many people often avoid asking questions in meetings due to fear of judgment, lack of confidence, or intimidation by authority figures.

Some fear their questions might appear trivial or reveal gaps in their knowledge, while others feel compelled to stay silent to align with the group when no one else speaks up.

Cultural norms and fear of negative repercussions can also discourage participation. In some cases, individuals assume others already understand the material, making them hesitant to ask for clarification. Let's understand how asking questions can help one in career.

Suresh's story

Suresh was a diligent employee in the marketing department of a mid-sized company. He was a hard worker and always delivered his tasks on time, but during staff and project meetings, he rarely spoke up.

He had questions about certain project objectives and marketing strategies, but he feared that asking might make him look less capable or unprepared in front of his boss and co-workers. So, Suresh would sit quietly, jot down notes, and try to figure out the details on his own afterward.

Over time, Suresh began to fall behind. Key aspects of the projects were unclear to him, which led to mistakes in his work that required revisions and ate into his time. While his colleagues progressed smoothly, Suresh found himself working late hours to catch up, often missing opportunities to contribute to new projects. His confidence took a hit, and he started feeling isolated in his role.

Matt's story

Matt, a project manager in the same company, took a different approach. In meetings, whether staff or project-related, Matt wasn't afraid to ask questions—whether about a vague instruction, an unclear deadline, or the rationale behind a new strategy.

Some of his questions even sparked discussions that led the team to refine their ideas and processes. Matt's willingness to ask questions not only helped him, but also benefited the entire team by ensuring everyone remained aligned.

As he continued to ask the right questions and offer insights, Matt gained a reputation for his thoroughness and ability to foresee potential challenges before they became real problems. His manager started relying on him for more complex projects and would often invite him to strategy meetings where his questions and input were valued. His colleagues, too, began to approach him for advice on how to improve their own tasks, recognizing his strong grasp of the project's goals and details.

As a result of his proactive approach, Matt was soon promoted to lead larger, high-visibility projects and his career flourished because he wasn't afraid to ask questions, which helped him stay informed, avoid mistakes, and demonstrate his leadership qualities.

Final thoughts:

Asking questions during staff or project meetings can significantly contribute to career progression in various ways.

It demonstrates engagement and interest in the discussion, showing your commitment to the organization and your desire to contribute meaningfully. Thoughtful questions also showcase critical thinking and problem-solving skills, which are highly valued for leadership roles. Additionally, seeking clarification ensures a better understanding of tasks and expectations, reducing errors and aligning you with the project's goals.

By speaking up, you build visibility and presence within the organization, making your contributions more noticeable to senior leadership.

Golden words: Questions are the keys that unlock understanding; the courage to ask them opens doors to progress.

—— •◇• ——

Surprise Bolt Strike!

Many employees, at the start of their careers or a new job, put in significant effort to secure a good position, driven by ambition and the desire for success. However, once they achieve stability, they may become complacent, prioritizing comfort over continuous growth.

This complacency often stems from a lack of ongoing challenges, a desire to maintain the status quo, or the belief that their skills are sufficient for future demands.

We have seen many waves of change in last three to four decades e.g., rise of PC, automation and now artificial intelligence.

If we look at the AI wave it is impacting everyone in the industry, it does not matter if you are a hardware engineer, software engineer, accountant or a doctor.

Suresh, a high-performing hardware systems engineer at a leading company in Bangalore, was satisfied with his work and career progress. However, over the past year, he began feeling increasingly uncomfortable due to the growing emphasis on AI-centric discussions and projects at his workplace. He struggled to accept the focus on AI within hardware engineering teams and felt that management was becoming less attentive to core engineering work.

As AI terms and concepts dominated team meetings, Suresh started to feel isolated, unable to follow what his colleagues were discussing. In the last 4-5 months, several high-priority projects emerged, and to his shock, he found himself excluded from them. This was a significant blow, as he had always been a key member of important projects, and the sudden shift left him feeling lost and concerned about his role in the company.

This abrupt shift in less than a year shattered Suresh's confidence, leaving him feeling adrift in an environment he once thrived in. As the realization sank in that he was no longer a valued contributor, a sense of urgency took hold. Haunted by the fear of being left behind in the AI revolution, he began to explore job opportunities outside the company, desperate to reclaim his sense of purpose and belonging.

Golden words: Change is inevitable; to succeed, it is essential to adapt and align ourselves in a timely manner.

————————— •◇• —————————

Day-34

Harnessing Lightning!

Change is the only constant; it continually occurs around us and affects everyone, whether directly or indirectly. This can be due to changing technologies, business environment, geo-political situation or something else.

Successful employees can often detect shifts within the company or industry and adapt to align with these changes. Adapting to change doesn't happen automatically; successful employees actively put in the effort to embrace new ideas and practices. They consciously work on this adaptation over time, and as they continue to practice it year after year, it gradually turns into a habit. Eventually, they may find themselves responding to new challenges and situations almost automatically, without even thinking about it. This ability to adapt becomes a natural part of their work life.

Matt was a hardworking and sincere employee with strong visibility and a good reputation among management.

A few years ago, workplace automation became a major topic of discussion, with nearly every company addressing it. Matt heard about it in several meetings as well. Although he was a hardware engineer, he didn't limit himself to his role or leave the responsibility to the software or automation teams. Instead, he began dedicating 40–50 minutes, two to three times a week, to learning how automation could be applied to hardware to improve efficiency. He read articles on what should be automated and how to estimate the return on investment (ROI) before pursuing automation projects.

During his research, Matt discovered that Python could be a valuable tool for his work, so he decided to invest in an online course and also attended a few internal training sessions offered by his company.

On weekends, he dedicated 4-5 hours to learning and practicing Python. Through his WhatsApp groups, he connected with some full-time automation experts and reached out to them for advice on speeding up his learning process. They shared useful tips, and Matt often turned to them for guidance whenever he had questions or faced challenges.

About two and a half months later, Matt's manager called a special meeting, asking the team to explore automation opportunities within their work.

He also asked them to determine the most suitable programming language for their automation needs.

After the manager finished speaking, Matt suggested that Python might be the right choice and explained his reasoning behind the recommendation. He proposed creating a list of potential tasks for automation, calculating the ROI for each, and then prioritizing them. Matt also offered to train other engineers and help them get up to speed with Python.

Impressed with Matt's initiative, the manager asked him to lead the team's automation efforts and provide weekly updates on their progress. He also encouraged other team members to collaborate with Matt. When the manager presented the team's automation plan to leadership, he took Matt along with him.

Over the next three years, Matt led two major automation projects while continuing to manage his regular responsibilities. One year after launching the automation initiatives, he received a promotion—an advancement he had initially anticipated in two to three years.

Golden words: Consistent, modest effort can steer your career forward, overcoming challenges brought by changes.

Up Hilling!

A large majority of employees express the desire to up skill themselves several times over the course of their careers. However, a significant number of them either fall short of fully achieving their goals or only manage to make partial progress.

In fact, some individuals abandon their plans before even getting started, as they perceive the process to be a daunting, uphill task. This occurs despite their understanding that acquiring new skills could greatly enhance their professional growth and open up more career opportunities in the long run.

Matt was a mechanical engineer at a company that designed medical equipment, which also involved electronic circuitry and software components. During design reviews and development phases, electronic and software engineers would join the discussions, and Matt often struggled to understand the terminology they used. This limited his ability to contribute beyond the mechanical aspects of the design. Determined to expand his knowledge, Matt decided to learn more about electronics and software engineering to enhance his understanding and involvement in the broader design process.

Feeling overwhelmed by the extensive syllabus he needed to cover, Matt decided to seek advice from his mentor, whom he regarded as an expert in multiple fields. After their discussion, Matt took the following steps:

Started micro learning: He broke down each topic into further smaller chunks that fit into short period of time. Instead of dedicating hours to courses, he spent just 20-30 minutes a day learning a new concept.

Leveraged work projects: He consistently connected the topic to his own projects, asking relevant questions both during and outside of formal meetings to deepen his understanding. For instance, after one meeting, he asked his electronics engineer colleague what type of motor they were using and the reasoning behind the choice. On another occasion, he inquired with his software colleague about the rationale for selecting a particular programming language.

Peer Learning and collaborations: Matt's company had several domain-specific groups focused on discussing innovations and the latest technologies, such as electronics innovation groups and software innovation groups. He asked his electronics engineer friend if he could join one of these groups. During the discussions, he contributed mechanical insights, which the group members found valuable, appreciating his involvement. Meanwhile, he learned a lot by listening to their conversations. Occasionally, topics from this group would surface in project meetings, where he felt more confident and comfortable. At times, he would share his mechanical expertise or be asked to provide his views, as he had already conducted mechanical analyses as part of the group discussions.

Used work sponsored learning: The Company offered various in-house training programs, and Matt began registering for electronics and software courses that he believed would benefit him.

Started lunch and learn: Matt made good friends in other domains and began having lunch with them. During these lunches, they often discussed industry trends and market situations, which significantly increased his awareness of other fields and helped him, feel more comfortable.

Started mindful learning: Matt started taking one or two days off every four to five months, strategically scheduling them next to weekends or holidays to create an extended four-five days break. He utilized this extra time for focused learning, dedicating himself to completing specific topics or online courses that he had been interested in. This approach allowed him to immerse himself in the material without distractions, enhancing his knowledge and skills in a structured manner.

Kept a record: Matt maintained a journal to document his progress and take notes on various topics he was studying. In addition to recording his thoughts, he made it a point to include the sources of his information. This practice not only helped him organize his learning but also ensured that he could easily refer back to the material later when he needed to revise or refresh his understanding.

Matt showed remarkable consistency in his efforts over a two-year period, which allowed his progress to become increasingly visible to his manager and the entire management chain. He developed a strong sense of confidence during discussions, contributing meaningfully and engaging with his colleagues. His extensive knowledge and impactful contributions earned him recognition as a strong contender for a future technical leadership position within the company.

Golden words: Up skilling isn't just an option; it's the only path to staying relevant.

Final Story

In the bustling city of Gurgaon (Gurugram), a major business hub in the National Capital Region of Delhi, Robert had carefully built a comfortable life as a marketing specialist at Superwave Systems. After years of hard work, countless late nights, and a steady climb up the corporate ladder, he had earned a coveted spot on an elite team. Promotions came effortlessly, and his career seemed to glide forward seamlessly. Proud of his achievements, Robert often shared his successes with friends and family, who admired his steady ascent within the company. With each new milestone, his confidence soared, leaving him feeling almost invincible. Yet, as the months turned into years, a quiet sense of complacency began to creep in—one he hadn't fully acknowledged.

Robert found himself slipping into a predictable, monotonous routine. Each day seemed to blend into the next, with the same meetings, the same strategies, and the same comfortable conversations with familiar faces. He completed his tasks efficiently and on time, but without putting in any extra effort or creativity. He had even started skipping industry webinars that he used to attend religiously, reassuring himself that his years of experience would be enough to carry him forward.

His colleagues seemed to be on the same path—drifting along in the same current, equally content with the stability they had worked hard to achieve. They would often joke about their comfortable positions, and Robert convinced himself that as long as he met his deadlines, maintained good rapport with his boss, and performed adequately, he would be fine. After all, change in their industry had always been slow-moving, and he felt safe in his position.

That comforting sense of security, however, was abruptly shattered one fateful morning. Superwave Systems announced a major restructuring initiative aimed at embracing a full-scale digital transformation. New technologies were set to be integrated into their marketing strategies, requiring all employees to adapt quickly in order to stay relevant in the evolving market. Robert and his colleagues gathered for an all-hands meeting where the CEO unveiled a strategic plan to pivot toward AI and data-driven marketing approaches, leaving many employees in shock. Whispers of uncertainty spread through the room, and as Robert observed his co-workers' pale, anxious faces, he felt a knot form in his stomach. A wave of dread washed over him as the reality began to set in—his once comfortable world was about to change in ways he had not anticipated.

As the weeks unfolded, Robert watched as his teammates scrambled to acquire new skills and adapt to the rapidly changing environment. Webinars, workshops, and training sessions became part of their daily routine. The once-familiar office buzzed with discussions about artificial intelligence, analytics, and cutting-edge marketing tools. However, while many of his colleagues were quick to dive into the challenge, Robert felt paralyzed. He hadn't invested time in learning these emerging technologies, and what once felt like a comfortable and secure position now felt increasingly precarious.

Initially, he tried to convince himself that this was just a passing storm—a temporary phase that would eventually blow over. But as days turned into weeks, Robert found himself drowning in a growing sea of uncertainty. His colleagues thrived in their new roles, taking on exciting projects that demonstrated their adaptability and enthusiasm for the changes. Meanwhile, Robert felt like an outsider, watching from the sidelines, struggling to keep up with the pace. It felt like the vibrant atmosphere of collaboration he once cherished had transformed into a painful reminder of his own failures. Each meeting was filled with laughter and camaraderie among his colleagues, a reminder that he no longer belonged to that circle of confident, forward-thinking professionals.

Robert's frustration gradually evolved into deep-seated fear. He would sit at his desk with a racing heart, watching his colleagues engage effortlessly with the new systems and technologies. Their eyes lit up with excitement as they took on new challenges, while Robert felt like every attempt he made to learn something new was like scaling an impossibly steep mountain.

His confidence plummeted, and he started dreading performance reviews with his manager. He knew deep down that he was no longer the top performer he had once been. Instead, he was struggling to stay afloat in the sea of rapid change.

In one particularly brutal meeting, Robert received feedback that hit him like a punch to the gut. His manager, though sympathetic, expressed concern about his inability to adapt. "Robert, we need everyone on board with these changes. The industry is evolving quickly, and we can't afford to be left behind," she said, her tone firm yet calm. Those words echoed in Robert's mind, amplifying his growing sense of failure and regret, and leaving him unsure of how to move forward.

Feeling utterly defeated, Robert decided to reach out to Mark, a mentor widely admired within the company. Colleagues often spoke highly of Mark, sharing how his guidance and encouragement had helped them overcome challenges and achieve their goals. Intrigued by these stories and desperate for clarity, Robert felt Mark might be the person to help him find a way forward. With a mix of hope and apprehension, he reached out, hoping for the support he desperately needed.

They met for coffee at a small café that overlooked the city skyline. As Robert poured out his frustrations, he felt vulnerable for the first time in years, with tears brimming in his eyes. Mark listened attentively, his face a mixture of concern and understanding. Once Robert finished, Mark leaned forward and said, "Robert, it's so easy to get comfortable when things are going well. But change is inevitable, especially in this industry. You have to stay curious and open to learning, even when it feels overwhelming. This could be your opportunity to rise from the ashes."

Mark's words stayed with Robert long after their meeting, and they slowly sparked a change in his mindset. Determined to rebuild his confidence, Robert enrolled in several online courses, dedicating hours each day to mastering new skills, even when his motivation faltered. He began to seek help from his more tech-savvy colleagues, who were more than willing to include him in their study groups. Night after night, Robert sat at his kitchen table, surrounded by textbooks and online tutorials, with the glow of his laptop lighting up his face as he pushed through the feelings of inadequacy. It was a challenging and humbling journey, filled with late nights, doubts, and the lingering fear that he might never catch up.

As the months passed, Robert slowly began to see a glimmer of hope. He gradually regained his confidence, implementing small but meaningful changes and showing initiative during team discussions. He raised his hand to contribute ideas in meetings, and, little by little, he emerged from the shadow of self-doubt. No longer just a bystander, Robert became an active participant in the company's transformation efforts.

Then, one day, the opportunity he had been working toward finally arrived. Superwave was preparing to launch a groundbreaking new marketing campaign for a cutting-edge product, and they needed a team leader to oversee the project. Armed with a blend of newly acquired technical skills and his natural marketing creativity, Robert seized the moment. He pitched innovative ideas that integrated data analytics with his marketing insights, captivating both his colleagues and management.

When the project launched, it exceeded all expectations, earning praise from clients and stakeholders alike. As Robert stood in front of the team, watching the fruits of their labour come to life, he felt a deep sense of pride and accomplishment. The journey had been anything but easy, but it had transformed him into a resilient, adaptable professional capable of thriving in a constantly evolving industry.

Reflecting on his earlier complacency, Robert realized that while the waves of change had initially swept him off his feet, they had ultimately propelled him toward a brighter, more fulfilling future. He had learned that growth is not simply about reaching a destination but about embracing the journey—one filled with challenges, setbacks, and triumphs. As he gazed out at the city skyline from the same café where he had once sought Mark's advice, Robert understood that in the fast-paced world of technology, remaining curious and open to learning would forever be his greatest asset.

———————— •◇• ————————

www.ingramcontent.com/pod-product-compliance
Lightning Source LLC
Chambersburg PA
CBHW031150130726
47988CB00006B/2621